KU-541-760

COULD A MONKEY WATERSKI?

...and other questions

Aleksei Bitskoff &
Camilla de la Bédoyère

QED

Capuchin monkeys are clever animals.

Design: Duck Egg Blue
Editor: Carly Madden
Editorial Director: Victoria Garrard
Art Director: Laura Roberts-Jensen
Publisher: Maxime Boucknooghe

Copyright © QED Publishing 2016

First published in the UK in 2016 by
QED Publishing
Part of The Quarto Group
The Old Brewery
6 Blundell Street
London N7 9BH

www.qed-publishing.co.uk

All rights reserved. No part of this publication may be reproduced, stored in a retrieval system, or transmitted in any form or by any means, electronic, mechanical, photocopying, recording, or otherwise, without the prior permission of the publisher, nor be otherwise circulated in any form of binding or cover other than that in which it is published and without a similar condition being imposed on the subsequent purchaser.

A catalogue record for this book is available from the British Library.

ISBN 978 1 78493 606 8

Printed in China

...at live in the jungle.

They have cheeky faces,
furry bodies and long tails
for gripping onto branches.

Imagine if a monkey
came to stay. Would she
have a fun time?

What if a monkey went into a noodle bar?

She would eat **oodles of noodles.**

A monkey could use chopsticks because she has fingers and thumbs!

But she would cover her food with spiders, ants and **crabs**. She loves eating crunchy bugs, fruit, seeds and juicy green leaves in the jungle.

Would a monkey enjoy sports day?

She would win the hurdles...

...and the long jump.

Monkeys can leap up to 3 metres when they are racing through trees.

That's like a human jumping more than 16 metres – or right over a bus!

Would a monkey enjoy bathtime?

Monkeys **love** water, so she'd have
a great time jumping into the bath!

SPLASH!

Monkeys often live in trees that grow alongside rivers, or the sea. When they get too hot they enjoy a cooling dip in the water.

SPLOSH!

Monkeys are great swimmers! They use their arms and legs to do the doggy-paddle.

Could a monkey help with the housework?

She could help to hang out the washing,

but she'd prefer to use the washing line

o have some **fun!**

In the wild, monkeys swing from branch to branch. Each swing can carry them several metres.

She can even hang **upside down** using her strong tail.

Could a monkey waterski?

A monkey could waterski the **right way**...

...and the **wrong way!**

She can grip with her feet as well as her hands because her big toes work like thumbs.

Would a monkey like to have her hair brushed?

No, she would prefer to have **smelly stuff** rubbed into it instead!

Insects often bite or sting monkeys, so monkeys cover themselves with squashed fruit and leaves, onions, mud or bugs to keep the pests away.

Some monkeys even coat their fur **with wee!**

Would a monkey like to go to school?

She would **love** being in school.
Monkeys can learn, just like children!

Her favourite lesson would be **science**.

She would have fun mixing colours, stirring potions and making bubbles.

POP!

Monkeys are curious, clever animals. In the jungle, they like to explore, play and discover new things.

Would a monkey have fun at the fair?

Yes, she would easily win a coconut at the coconut shy.

In the jungle, monkeys sit in trees and throw **fruit, nuts** and **branches** at animals below!

She would show everyone how **STRONG** she is!

Monkeys use **big stones** to hit nuts and **CRACK** them open.

DING!

Would a monkey sleep in a bed?

No, she would sleep **on top of the wardrobe!**

In her jungle home she sleeps in the treetops, where she is safe from **big hungry animals**, such as jaguars and crocodiles!

She won't need a blanket because her **thick fur** will keep her warm.

But she might like a teddy to cuddle. Monkeys live in families, and they love **snuggly hugs!**

More about capuchin monkeys

Monkey is pointing to the place where she lives.
Can you see where you live?

FACT FILE

Capuchin monkeys live in trees and only come to the ground to drink water, grab food or play.

Monkeys live in family groups, called troops. There can be 30 monkeys or more in a troop.

Capuchins can twitch their eyebrows to communicate their feelings!

Monkeys help the rainforest to grow. They eat fruits and the seeds pass through the monkeys' bodies, ready to start growing into plants and trees.

Monkeys have tails but apes (gorillas, chimps and orang-utans) are tail-less.

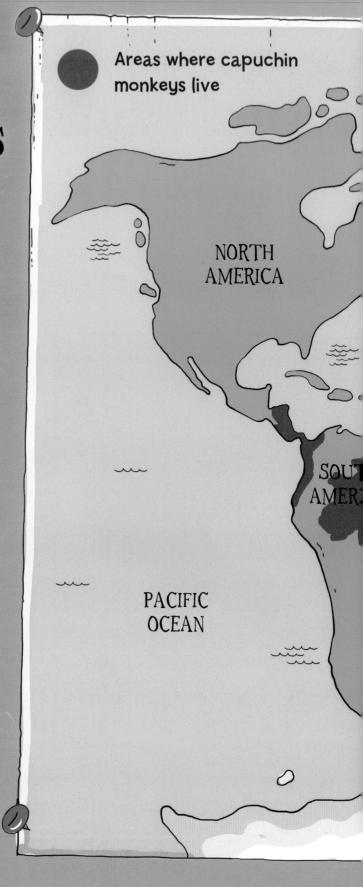

Areas where capuchin monkeys live

NORTH AMERICA

SOUTH AMERICA

PACIFIC OCEAN

Greetings from South America!

POST CARD

I am writing this to you from the top of my favourite tree, looking over the river and watching a scary crocodile below! I have been throwing some nuts at him but he hasn't spotted me yet. Ha ha!

Come and visit me in the jungle some time.

Your best friend, Monkey   X

SENT BY CAPUCHIN POST
TREETOPS, BRAZIL

1ST

The Wild Family
189 Treetop Avenue
Chester
CH13 4FH
UK

8713263560583674519